IRISH SONGS FOR GUITAR

by **DANNY CARNAHAN**

Editor: Jeffrey Pepper Rodgers

Cover photograph: Rory Earnshaw

Author photograph: Saundra Wane

ISBN 978-0-634-06410-4

STRING LETTER PUBLISHING

EXCLUSIVELY DISTRIBUTED BY

HAL•LEONARD®
CORPORATION

7777 W. BLUEMOUND RD. P.O. BOX 13819 MILWAUKEE, WI 53213

Visit Hal Leonard Online at
www.halleonard.com

In Australia Contact:
Hal Leonard Australia Pty. Ltd.
22 Taunton Drive P.O. Box 5130
Cheltenham East, 3192 Victoria, Australia
Email: ausadmin@halleonard.com

CONTENTS

INTRODUCTION

One summer in my teens I was visiting family in the far west of Wales. My young cousins and I spent evenings tuned into a pirate radio station, Radio Caroline, which broadcast very cool music from a ship out in the Irish Sea, just out of the BBC's reach. Drawn by the rebellious spirit of the station, I was captivated by what I heard: the Irish hit parade of 1968. I'd never given much thought to Irish music as distinct from any other tradition, but I fell instantly and deeply in love with the entire playlist. I managed to find a couple of LPs in heavy rotation, the Dubliners' *Seven Drunken Nights* and Danny Doyle's *Whiskey on a Sunday*. A few months later, about the time a bankrupt Radio Caroline was hauled off the air, I was back home in California, learning every song on both albums by heart. Three decades later, those songs are still happily rolling around in my brain.

There is no richer lyrical tradition than the one that gave birth to Irish ballads and folk songs. Every conceivable human activity, emotional state, adventure, and misadventure experienced by the Irish, individually and collectively, has been artfully captured in countless songs that are so catchy and memorable, they'll be sung as long as people have vocal cords. And one doesn't have to be Irish to feel the emotional power of the love songs and the hopeful pride that fuels the best historical ballads.

I've collected 15 of my favorite Irish songs for this book, choosing from hundreds I love every bit as much. I tried to cover as many moods and subjects as practical in the available space. So we have innocent (and very old) love songs like "Rosemary Fair" and more lustful romps like "Newry Town." We have the revolutionary fervor of "The Rising of the Moon" in contrast to the story of the poor kid who deserts after one day in the army in "The Rambler from Clare." We have the regional pride of "The Star of the County Down" and the terrible longing for home in "Paddy's Green Shamrock Shore." And then there's highway robbery, questionable job choices, unabashed love for one's fellow man, and more.

Most of these songs predate the music hall era of the early 20th century, which stuck us with some regrettably stereotyped hits that are all too available elsewhere. I tried to dig a little deeper into the current oral tradition for songs that enjoy some popularity and for settings that fall pleasantly under the fingers on the guitar. These songs use three tunings—standard, dropped-D (with the sixth string tuned down to D), and the less common D A D D A D—and the various right-hand techniques should come pretty easily to anyone who's played fingerstyle guitar. Most songs can be played with thumb and two fingers, though there are some nice chord rolls using three fingers. Using the fingers both to pick upward and snap downward on the nails might be challenging at first, but it's really no harder than banjo frailing. And sometimes I just brace my index finger with my thumb for my "zen pick." Overall, I've tried to keep things pared down to essentials because I don't want to work hard any more than you do.

The songs in this collection can be heard in pubs across Ireland and in sessions in every outpost of the English-speaking world. And this is just the tiniest sample of what's out there. You could learn a new Irish song every week and not exhaust the tradition. So here's hoping you take as much delight in these songs as I do and find yourself hungering for more.

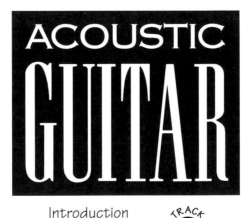

Introduction and Tune-Up: Standard Tuning

TRACK 1

Need help with the songs in this book? Ask a question in our free, on-line support forum in the Guitar Talk section of www.acousticguitar.com.

MUSIC NOTATION KEY

The music in this book is written in standard notation and tablature. Here's how to read it.

STANDARD NOTATION

Standard notation is written on a five-line staff. Notes are written in alphabetical order from A to G.

The duration of a note is determined by three things: the note head, stem, and flag. A whole note (𝅝) equals four beats. A half note (𝅗𝅥) is half of that: two beats. A quarter note (𝅘𝅥) equals one beat, an eighth note (𝅘𝅥𝅮) equals half of one beat, and a 16th note (𝅘𝅥𝅯) is a quarter beat (there are four 16th notes per beat).

The fraction (4/4, 3/4, 6/8, etc.) or c character shown at the beginning of a piece of music denotes the time signature. The top number tells you how many beats are in each measure, and the bottom number indicates the rhythmic value of each beat (4 equals a quarter note, 8 equals an eighth note, 16 equals a 16th note, and 2 equals a half note). The most common time signature is 4/4, which signifies four quarter notes per measure and is sometimes designated with the symbol c (for common time). The symbol ¢ stands for cut time (2/2). Most songs are either in 4/4 or 3/4.

TABLATURE

In tablature, the six horizontal lines represent the six strings of the guitar, with the first string on the top and sixth on the bottom. The numbers refer to fret numbers on a given string. The notation and tablature in this book are designed to be used in tandem—refer to the notation to get the rhythmic information and note durations, and refer to the tablature to get the exact locations of the notes on the guitar fingerboard.

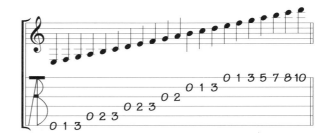

FINGERINGS

Fingerings are indicated with small numbers and letters in the notation. Fretting-hand fingering is indicated with 1 for the index finger, 2 the middle, 3 the ring, 4 the pinky, and *T* the thumb. Picking-hand fingering is indicated by *i* for the index finger, *m* the middle, *a* the ring, *c* the pinky, and *p* the thumb. Remember that the fingerings indicated are only suggestions; if you find a different way that works better for you, use it.

BACK SNAPS

Several transcriptions in this collection indicate back-snap hits with the fingernails of the index and middle fingers using a down-pointing arrow. Playing these arrangements with both the front and back of the fingers is important in capturing the Celtic lilt. I don't insist on the explosive back snap that Martin Simpson or Steve Baughman have made such strong elements of their styles. But getting confident with the solid back snap will help train a hand position ideally suited for many more Irish and Celtic song and tune settings.

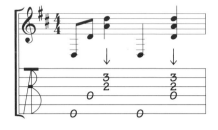

CAPOS

If a capo is used, a Roman numeral indicates the fret where the capo should be placed. The standard notation and tablature is written as if the capo were the nut of the guitar. For instance, a tune capoed anywhere up the neck and played using key-of-G chord shapes and fingerings will be written in the key of G. Likewise, open strings held down by the capo are written as open strings.

TUNINGS

Alternate guitar tunings are given from the lowest (sixth) string to the highest (first) string. For instance, D A D G B E indicates standard tuning with the bottom string dropped to D. Standard notation for songs in alternate tunings always reflects the actual pitches of the notes. Arrows underneath tuning notes indicate strings that are altered from standard tuning and whether they are tuned up or down.

VOCAL TUNES

Vocal tunes are sometimes written with a fully tabbed-out introduction and a vocal melody with chord diagrams for the rest of the piece. The tab intro is usually your indication of which strum or fingerpicking pattern to use in the rest of the piece. The melody with lyrics underneath is the melody sung by the vocalist. Occasionally smaller notes are written with the melody to indicate the harmony part sung by another vocalist. These are not to be confused with cue notes, which are small notes that indicate melodies that vary when a section is repeated. Listen to a recording of the piece to get a feel for the guitar accompaniment and to hear the singing if you aren't skilled at reading vocal melodies.

ARTICULATIONS

There are a number of ways you can articulate a note on the guitar. Notes connected with slurs (not to be confused with ties) in the tablature or standard notation are articulated with either a hammer-on, pull-off, or slide. Lower notes

slurred to higher notes are played as hammer-ons; higher notes slurred to lower notes are played as pull-offs. While it's usually obvious that slurred notes are played as hammer-ons or pull-offs, an *H* or *P* is included above the tablature as an extra reminder.

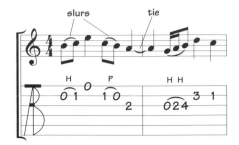

Slides are represented with a dash, and an *S* is included above the tab. A dash preceding a note represents a slide into the note from an indefinite point in the direction of the slide; a dash following a note indicates a slide off of the note to an indefinite point in the direction of the slide. For two slurred notes connected with a slide, you should pick the first note and then slide into the second.

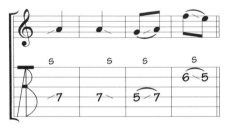

Bends are represented with upward curves, as shown in the next example. Most bends have a specific destination pitch—the number above the bend symbol shows how much the bend raises the string's pitch: ¼ for a slight bend, ½ for a half step, 1 for a whole step.

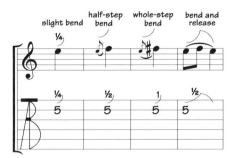

CHORD ROLLS

A vertical wavy line indicates a chord roll played with thumb and either two or three fingers. This differs from a straight chord with all notes played simultaneously. The thumb hits an instant before the index finger, which hits an instant before the middle finger, and so on. The chord occupies the same time value as a straight chord but sounds more harplike and flowing.

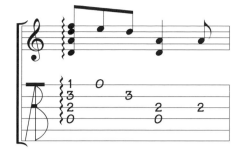

REPEATS

One of the most confusing parts of a musical score can be the navigation symbols, such as repeats, *D.S. al Coda, D.C. al Fine, To Coda,* etc.

Repeat symbols are placed at the beginning and end of the passage to be repeated.

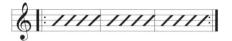

You should ignore repeat symbols with the dots on the right side the first time you encounter them; when you come to a repeat symbol with dots on the left side, jump back to the previous repeat symbol facing the opposite direction (if there is no previous symbol, go to the beginning of the piece). The next time you come to the repeat symbol, ignore it and keep going unless it includes instructions such as "Repeat three times."

Often a section will often have a different ending after each repeat. The example below includes a first and a second ending. Play until you hit the repeat symbol, jump back to the previous repeat symbol and play until you reach the bracketed first ending, skip the measures under the bracket and jump immediately to the second ending, and then continue.

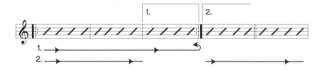

D.S. stands for *dal segno* or "from the sign." When you encounter this indication, jump immediately to the sign (𝄋). *D.S.* is usually accompanied by *al Fine* or *al Coda*. *Fine* indicates the end of a piece. A coda is a final passage near the end of a piece and is indicated with ⊕. *D.S. al Coda* simply tells you to jump back to the sign and continue on until you are instructed to jump to the coda, indicated with *To Coda* ⊕.

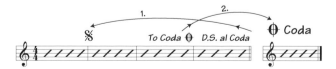

D.C. stands for *da capo* or "from the beginning." Jump to the top of the piece when you encounter this indication.

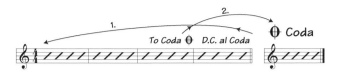

D.C. al Fine tells you to jump to the beginning of a tune and continue until you encounter the *Fine* indicating the end of the piece (ignore the *Fine* the first time through).

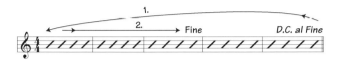

A WORD ABOUT D A D D A D TUNING

I decided to include a couple of songs in this rather odd tuning for two reasons. First, I've loved both songs dearly for over 20 years. Second, early in my Irish travels I learned how much fun very drony tunings could be. Many sessions featured Irish bouzoukis tuned open to G D G D or A E A E. I often found that the drone strings created powerful tensions against the sung melodies. Dublin singer/guitarist Kieran Halpin may have been my initial inspiration for this tuning in the late '70s, though too many pints accompanied that apprenticeship for me to be sure. While touring with Caswell Carnahan in the early '80s I kept one guitar dedicated to D A D D A D, replacing the G string with another D string to compensate for the one downside of this tuning: that the unison strings are difficult to keep in tune above the fifth fret if their diameters are different. But try it anyway with whatever strings you've got, and see if you like the open chord voicings you can't get in standard or dropped-D tuning.

When accompanying songs in D A D D A D, I don't strive for quite the same level of right-hand accuracy as I do in other tunings. This is mostly because I want the guitar to do as much lovely open-string work as possible. In my notation, I've indicated the strings I emphasize most, but this doesn't mean you want to avoid or dampen the other strings. Quite the contrary. As long as you're hitting the low D or G or A to help establish the chord changes, pretty much any other string is fair game. As for the right-hand pattern, whether you choose to use a pick or the back of your index finger, both songs share a very steady down-up pattern, so that if you count out "1 and, 2 and, 3 and" all the numbered strokes will be downstrokes (toward the floor) and all the *ands* will be upstrokes (toward the ceiling). Occasionally you'll go down or up without making contact with any string, but do keep this pattern going, as it works wonders in propelling the song forward.

ROSEMARY FAIR

Though I first ran across this song in Colm O Lochlainn's *More Irish Street Ballads*, the sweetest and most memorable rendering I've ever heard is on Mick Hanly's 1976 album *A Kiss in the Morning Early* (Mulligan 005). I chose a very simple picking pattern for this song to maintain the gentle waltz rhythm while never straying too far from the melody. I've heard the song sung many times in pubs and folk clubs, with the singers often leaving out as many as half the verses. I've provided the whole story here, so you can decide how much of it to tell and whether or not to give equal time to both sides in this possibly testy, possibly tongue-in-cheek lover's quarrel. Since it's a long ballad without a chorus to break up the melody line, you

might want to play the tune through instrumentally every three verses or so. Or vamp on a simple C arpeggio for two bars before starting the next verse. Or play it straight through as written. It will retain its sweet, plaintive quality however you decide to go.

One tiny structural note: While this song is counted in 6/8, you'll notice that the seventh bar is in 9/8. This is a common trait in many traditional songs from all over the British Isles. The emphasis might shift forward or backward a beat in order to tell the story more conversationally. Mostly this will happen without you even noticing it . . . as I didn't notice it in this song until I wrote out the notation. Don't let it worry you.

1. YOU MAY GO DOWN TO ROSEMARY FAIR
   EVERY ROSE GROWS MERRY AND FINE
   PICK ME OUT THEN THE FINEST BOY THERE
   I WILL MAKE HIM A TRUE LOVER OF MINE

2. TELL HIM TO GET ME AN ACRE OF LAND
   EVERY ROSE GROWS MERRY AND FINE
   BETWEEN THE SALT SEA AND THE SALT SEA STRAND
   OR HE CANNOT BE A TRUE LOVER OF MINE

3. TELL HIM TO PLOW IT WITH A RAM'S HORN
   EVERY ROSE GROWS MERRY AND FINE
   AND SOW IT ALL OVER WITH ONE GRAIN OF CORN
   OR HE CANNOT BE A TRUE LOVER OF MINE

4. TELL HIM TO REAP IT WITH A COCK'S FEATHER
   EVERY ROSE GROWS MERRY AND FINE
   AND BIND IT ALL ROUND WITH STRAPPINGS OF LEATHER
   AND I WILL MAKE HIM A TRUE LOVER OF MINE

5. TELL HIM TO DRAW IT HOME ON A SNAIL
   EVERY ROSE GROWS MERRY AND FINE
   AND THRESH IT ALL OUT WITH A MOUSIE'S TAIL
   AND I WILL MAKE HIM A TRUE LOVER OF MINE

6. TELL HIM TO BRING IT TO ROSEMARY FAIR
   EVERY ROSE GROWS MERRY AND FINE
   AND WHEN HE ARRIVES THERE'LL BE NOBODY THERE
   AND HE CANNOT BE A TRUE LOVER OF MINE

7. SINCE YOU HAVE BEEN SO HARD UPON ME
   EVERY ROSE GROWS MERRY AND FINE
   I'M GOING TO BE AS HARD UPON THEE
   IF YOU WISH TO BE A TRUE LOVER OF MINE

8. YOU MAY GO DOWN TO ROSEMARY FAIR
   EVERY ROSE GROWS MERRY AND FINE
   AND PICK ME OUT THE NICEST GIRL THERE
   AND I WILL MAKE HER A TRUE LOVER OF MIN

9. TELL HER TO SEND ME A CAMBERIC SHIRT
   EVERY ROSE GROWS MERRY AND FINE
   MADE WITHOUT NEEDLE OR A NEEDLE'S WORK
   OR SHE CANNOT BE A TRUE LOVER OF MINE

10. TELL HER TO WASH IT IN YONDER WELL
    EVERY ROSE GROWS MERRY AND FINE
    WHERE WATER NE'ER ROSE NOR RAIN NEVER FELL
    AND I WILL MAKE HER A TRUE LOVER OF MINE

11. TELL HER TO DRY IT ON YONDER THORN
    EVERY ROSE GROWS MERRY AND FINE
    WHERE NONE EVER GREW SINCE ADAM WAS BORN
    AND I WILL MAKE HER A TRUE LOVER OF MINE

    [REPEAT FIRST VERSE]

THE RISING OF THE MOON

What collection of Irish songs would be complete without a rebel song? A tale of the 1798 Irish rising, "The Rising of the Moon" was written about the time of the American Civil War by a Mullingar Fenian named J. K. Casey, who died at the age of 24. Casey borrowed the melody from the air "Wearing of the Green," which is attributed to the 18th century blind harper Turlough O'Carolan. A classic version of this song can be heard on the Clancy Brothers' 1959 *The Rising of the Moon: Irish Songs of Rebellion* (Tradition 1066). In pub sessions these days you don't hear as many rollicking songs of revolution and gumption, but the tradition is so deep and the songs are so plentiful and singable that they're not likely to fade away entirely.

You'll notice that I often let the high E string ring open through the chord changes, even when it isn't part of the chord. I do this deliberately to add uneasy suspension to the chord progression and to avoid the overly sweet B7 chord with the high F# (second fret, first string). I also try to maintain a strong pulse on the downbeat of each bar while picking this song, even though I'm hitting most of the second beats with the sharp, downward snapping motion on the backs of my index and middle fingernails. I find this gives the arrangement a marching momentum that really suits the lyrics.

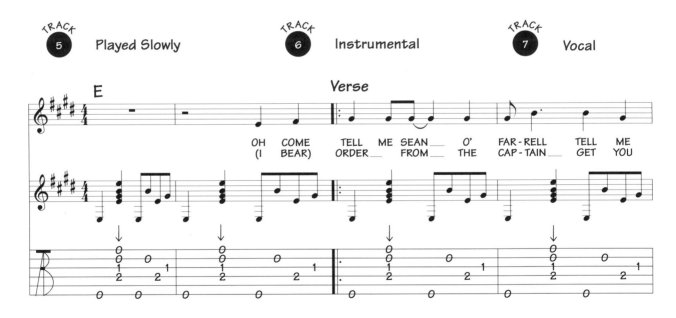

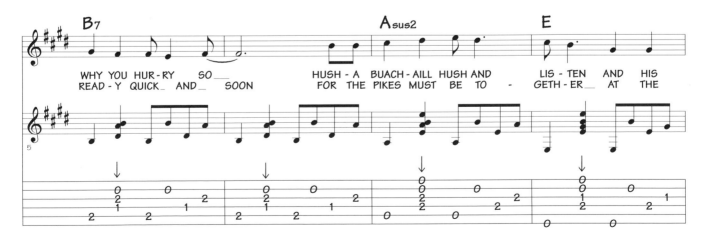

Chorus

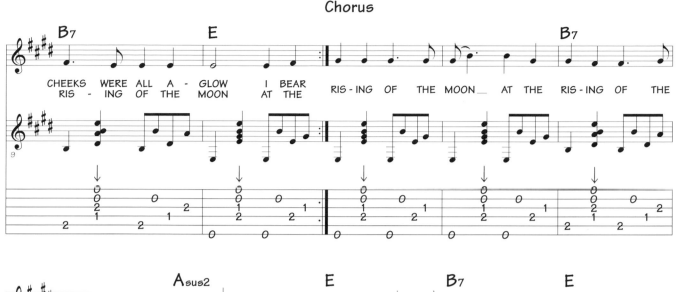

1. OH COME TELL ME SEAN O'FARRELL TELL ME WHY YOU HURRY SO
   HUSHA BUACHAILL* HUSH AND LISTEN AND HIS CHEEKS WERE ALL AGLOW
   I BEAR ORDERS FROM THE CAPTAIN GET YOU READY QUICK AND SOON
   FOR THE PIKES MUST BE TOGETHER AT THE RISING OF THE MOON

       AT THE RISING OF THE MOON AT THE RISING OF THE MOON
       FOR THE PIKES MUST BE TOGETHER AT THE RISING OF THE MOON

2. AND COME TELL ME SEAN O'FARRELL WHERE THE GATH'RIN IS TO BE
   AT THE OLD SPOT BY THE RIVER QUITE WELL KNOWN TO YOU AND ME
   ONE MORE WORD FOR SIGNAL TOKEN WHISTLE OUT THE MARCHIN' TUNE
   WITH YOUR PIKE UPON YOUR SHOULDER AT THE RISING OF THE MOON

       AT THE RISING OF THE MOON AT THE RISING OF THE MOON
       WITH YOUR PIKE UPON YOUR SHOULDER AT THE RISING OF THE MOON

3. OUT FROM MANY A MUD WALL CABIN EYES WERE WATCHING THROUGH THE NIGHT
   MANY A MANLY HEART WAS BEATING FOR THE COMING MORNING LIGHT
   MURMURS PASSED ALONG THE VALLEY LIKE THE BANSHEE'S LONELY CROON
   AND A THOUSAND PIKES WERE FLASHING AT THE RISING OF THE MOON

       AT THE RISING OF THE MOON AT THE RISING OF THE MOON
       AND A THOUSAND PIKES WERE FLASHING AT THE RISING OF THE MOON

4. DOWN BESIDE THAT SINGING RIVER THAT BLACK MASS OF MEN WAS SEEN
   HIGH ABOVE THEIR SHINING WEAPONS FLEW THEIR OWN BELOVED GREEN
   DEATH TO EVERY FOE AND TRAITOR! FORWARD STRIKE THE MARCHING TUNE
   AND HURRAH ME BOYS FOR FREEDOM 'TIS THE RISING OF THE MOON

       'TIS THE RISING OF THE MOON 'TIS THE RISING OF THE MOON
       AND HURRAH ME BOYS FOR FREEDOM 'TIS THE RISING OF THE MOON

*IRISH WORD MEANING "YOUNG UNMARRIED MAN."

BLACK VELVET BAND

This is one of the most popular Irish songs ever written. It's got just about everything in it: a gritty slice of life, some honest lustful intent, a pretty girl who's up to no good, a hapless hero who suffers at the hands of an unfair English court, and a trip to Australia. It could have been a PBS miniseries. It's also one of the most singable songs in this collection, as the chorus and the verses follow the same melody and chord changes. My recording on the CD accompanying this book is on the slow side for the sake of easier learning, but when I sing it in public, it rips right along. As in "The Rising of the Moon," make sure your downbeats are strong and even.

1. IN A NEAT LITTLE TOWN THEY CALL BELFAST
APPRENTICED TO TRADE I WAS BOUND
AND MANY'S THE HOUR SWEET HAPPINESS
I SPENT IN THAT NEAT LITTLE TOWN
A SAD MISFORTUNE CAME OVER ME
THAT CAUSED ME TO STRAY FROM THE LAND
FAR AWAY FROM MY FRIENDS AND RELATIONS
BETRAYED BY THE BLACK VELVET BAND

    HER EYES THEY SHONE LIKE DIAMONDS
    I THOUGHT HER THE QUEEN OF THE LAND
    AND HER HAIR IT HUNG OVER HER SHOULDERS
    TIED UP WITH A BLACK VELVET BAND

2. I TOOK A STROLL DOWN BROADWAY
MEANING NOT LONG FOR TO STAY
WHEN WHO SHOULD I MEET BUT THIS PRETTY FAIR MAID
A-TRAIPSIN' ALONG THE HIGHWAY
SHE WAS BOTH FAIR AND HANDSOME
HER NECK IT WAS JUST LIKE A SWAN
AND HER HAIR IT HUNG OVER HER SHOULDERS
TIED UP WITH A BLACK VELVET BAND

    CHORUS

3. I TOOK A STROLL WITH THIS PRETTY FAIR MAID
WHEN A GENTLEMAN PASSED US BY
I KNEW SHE MEANT THE DOIN' OF HIM
BY THE LOOK IN HER ROGUISH BLACK EYE
A GOLD WATCH SHE TOOK FROM HIS POCKET
AND PLACED IT RIGHT INTO MY HAND
AND THE VERY NEXT THING THAT I SAID WAS
BAD LUCK TO THE BLACK VELVET BAND*

    CHORUS

4. BEFORE THE JUDGE AND THE JURY
NEXT MORNING I HAD TO APPEAR
THE JUDGE HE SAID TO ME YOUNG MAN
YOUR CASE IT IS PROVEN CLEAR
WE'LL GIVE YOU SEVEN YEARS PENAL SERVITUDE
TO BE SPENT FAR AWAY FROM THE LAND
FAR AWAY FROM YOUR FRIENDS AND RELATIONS
BETRAYED BY THE BLACK VELVET BAND

    CHORUS

5. SO COME ALL YOU JOLLY YOUNG FELLOWS
A WARNING TAKE BY ME
WHEN YOU ARE OUT ON THE TOWN MY LADS
BEWARE OF THE PRETTY COLLEEN
SHE'LL FEED YOU WITH STRONG DRINK ME LADS
TILL YOU ARE UNABLE TO STAND
AND THE VERY NEXT THING THAT YOU'RE KNOWIN'
YOU'VE LANDED IN VAN DIEMAN'S LAND**

* OFTEN THIS LINE READS "BAD CESS TO THE BLACK VELVET BAND," AN OLD PHRASE MEANING
THE OPPOSITE OF SUCCESS, BUT I PREFER THE MORE CONTEMPORARY WORDING.
** AUSTRALIA.

WHISKEY IN THE JAR

Here's a song of highway robbery and romantic betrayal that's been popular for over 200 years. A song with real attitude, it's been performed by everybody from the Dubliners (*Irish Drinking Songs*, Columbia/Legacy 52833) to Metallica (*Garage, Inc.,* Elektra 62299) and shows no sign of fading from the pub scene. I try to work the story by using dynamics to drop down in the fourth verse, then build to the big finish. The fingerpicking pattern I use here allows for dynamic control, in that I can leave out the back-snap hits I play on the second beat of most bars, substitute a more even alternating picking pattern for the quieter passages, then return to the snap when I want maximum emphasis. Feel free to take this at a peppier clip than I use on the CD.

It's somewhat unclear where this little drama took place. For years I've sung the first line to include "the far Gilgarry mountains," blissfully unaware that I'd garbled the name back in my checkered youth. But I refuse to take too much blame, as there seem to be abundant variants besides mine. "Far famed Kerry mountains" and "Cork and Kerry mountains" are pretty fair candidates for accuracy. And Shane McGowan of the Pogues sang "Kilmagenny Mountains" even though the closest thing to Kilmagenny in Ireland is a Kilmaganny Parish in County Kilkenny. So take this song in the loose and forgiving form in which it's offered and pick whatever mountains seem best. Wherever it happened, though, that girl was a piece of work, wasn't she?

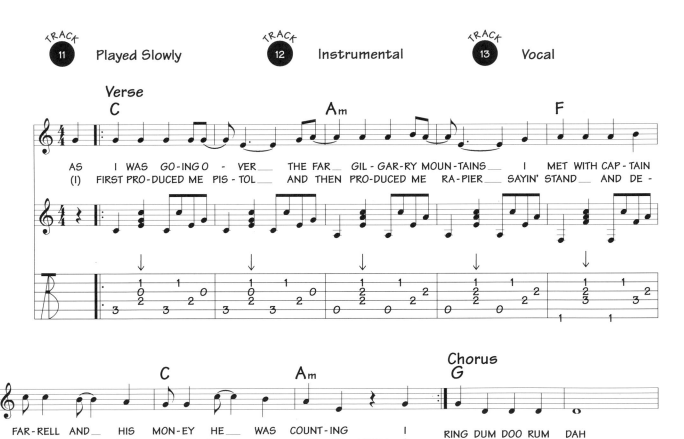

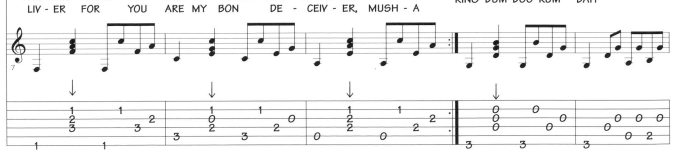

1. AS I WAS GOING OVER THE FAR GILGARRY MOUNTAINS
   I MET WITH CAPTAIN FARRELL AND HIS MONEY HE WAS COUNTING
   I FIRST PRODUCED ME PISTOL AND THEN PRODUCED ME RAPIER
   SAYIN' STAND AND DELIVER FOR YOU ARE MY BOLD DECEIVER

   MUSHA RING DUM DOO RUM DAH
   WHACK FOL THE DADDY OH
   WHACK FOL THE DADDY OH
   THERE'S WHISKEY IN THE JAR

2. I COUNTED OUT HIS MONEY AND IT MADE A PRETTY PENNY
   I PUT IT IN MY POCKET AND I TOOK IT HOME TO JENNY
   SHE SIGHED AND SHE SWORE THAT SHE NEVER WOULD BETRAY ME
   BUT THE DEVIL TAKE THE WOMEN FOR THEY NEVER CAN BE EASY

   CHORUS

3. I WENT INTO MY CHAMBER ALL FOR TO TAKE A SLUMBER
   I DREAMT OF GOLD AND JEWELS AND FOR SURE IT WAS NO WONDER
   BUT JENNY TOOK MY CHARGES AND SHE FILLED THEM UP WITH WATER
   THEN SENT FOR CAPTAIN FARRELL TO BE READY FOR THE SLAUGHTER

   CHORUS

4. IT WAS EARLY IN THE MORNING AS I ROSE UP FOR TRAVEL
   THE GUARDS WERE ALL AROUND ME AND LIKEWISE WAS CAPTAIN FARRELL
   I FIRST PRODUCED MY PISTOL FOR SHE STOLE AWAY MY RAPIER
   BUT I COULDN'T SHOOT THE WATER SO A PRISONER I WAS TAKEN

   CHORUS

5. AND IF ANYONE CAN AID ME IT'S MY BROTHER IN THE ARMY
   IF I CAN FIND HIS STATION BE IT CORK OR IN KILLARNEY
   AND IF HE'LL COME AND SAVE ME WE'LL GO ROVING IN KILKENNY
   I SWEAR HE'LL TREAT ME BETTER THAN ME DARLING SPORTING JENNY.

   CHORUS

6. NOW SOME MEN TAKE DELIGHT IN THE DRINKING AND THE ROVING
   BUT OTHERS TAKE DELIGHT IN THE GAMBLING AND THE SMOKING
   BUT I TAKE DELIGHT IN THE JUICE OF THE BARLEY
   AND COURTING PRETTY FAIR MAIDS IN THE MORNING BRIGHT AND EARLY

   CHORUS

THE STAR OF THE COUNTY DOWN

This, too, is one of Ireland's best-loved songs. For a vocal rendering, you can't do better than John McCormack's version, available on the three-CD set *Legendary Irish Tenor* (Goldies 25444). The tradition boasts hundreds of songs proclaiming the girls of a particular county or village or parish to be the most beautiful in the country, if not the world. And true or not, whoever wrote this sweet ballad really had it bad for his nut-brown Rose. It's set in a rolling 3/4 meter that gives plenty of room to the lyrics. This is one you don't want to take too fast. You'll notice on the CD that I only gave the first four-line verse before singing the chorus. Generally, the verses are paired up before each chorus, but

feel free to sing as many choruses as you like. The way the chorus blossoms into that bright G-major chord before resolving back to the minor never gets old for me.

Notice also that in the verse section I've notated the right-hand picking pattern very regular and plain, but in the last half of the chorus I show how you can catch the last eighth note in each bar as a transition note into the next chord. Some of these transition notes are part of the previous chord, some are open strings leading into the next chord. Use whichever finger seems most appropriate. You can, of course, mix these up to suit yourself once you're comfortable with the pattern.

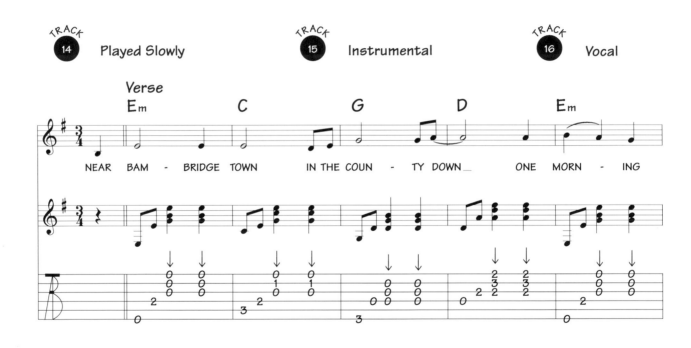

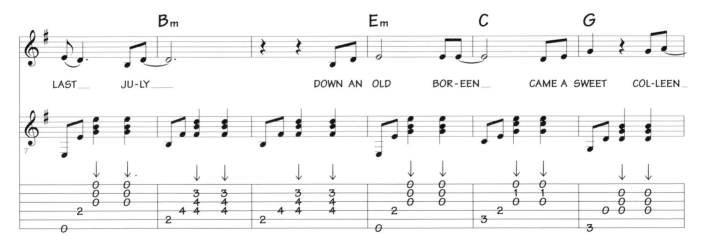

1. NEAR BAMBRIDGE TOWN IN THE COUNTY DOWN
   ONE MORNING LAST JULY
   DOWN AN OLD BOREEN CAME A SWEET COLLEEN
   AND SHE SMILED AS SHE PASSED ME BY

   SHE LOOKED SO SWEET FROM HER TWO BARE FEET
   TO THE CROWN OF HER NUT-BROWN HAIR
   SUCH A WINSOME ELF THAT I PINCHED MYSELF
   FOR TO SEE I WAS REALLY THERE

   FROM BANTRY BAY UP TO DERRY QUAY
   AND FROM GALWAY TO DUBLIN TOWN
   NO MAID I'VE SEEN LIKE THE BROWN COLLEEN
   THAT I MET AT THE COUNTY DOWN

2. AS SHE ONWARD SPED SURE I SHOOK MY HEAD
   AND I GAZED WITH A FEELING QUARE
   AND I SAID SAID I TO A PASSER-BY
   WHO'S THE MAID WITH THE NUT-BROWN HAIR?

   OH HE SMILED AT ME AND HE SAID TO ME
   THAT'S THE GEM OF IRELAND'S CROWN
   SHE'S YOUNG ROSIE MCCANN FROM THE BANKS OF THE BANN
   SHE'S THE STAR OF THE COUNTY DOWN

   CHORUS

3. AT THE HARVEST FAIR SHE'LL BE SURELY THERE
   SO I'LL DRESS IN MY SUNDAY CLOTHES
   WITH MY SHOES SHINED BRIGHT AND MY HAIR COCKED RIGHT
   FOR A SMILE FROM THE NUT-BROWN ROSE

   NO PIPE I'LL SMOKE NO HORSE I'LL YOKE
   TILL MY PLOW IS A NUT-COLORED BROWN
   TILL SMILING BRIGHT BY MY OWN FIRELIGHT
   SITS THE STAR OF THE COUNTY DOWN

   CHORUS

THE PARTING GLASS

There are few more powerful ways to end a musical evening than to sing "The Parting Glass." This song is so simple, direct, and honest it is sometimes hard to sing without choking up. You can find versions in all the best collections, including *Irish Street Ballads*, and you can hear it sung in every corner of the British Isles. Robin Williamson's performances of this song, accompanying himself on the harp (available on *Songs of Love and Parting and Five Bardic*

Mysteries, TMC 9403), more than once left me in hopeful tears. The rhythm is free, as I played on the CD, and you can take as much time as you like with each line, savoring it and letting the meaning just flow out. In fact, the more you keep a Celtic harp in the back of your mind while playing this song, the better it might sound. Let your arpeggios ring. And repeat the last line of the last verse to wrap it up.

ALL   I'VE__ DONE   FOR WANT   OF__ WIT   TO   MEM - ORY NOW   I __ CAN'T RE - CALL ____   SO__

__ FILL__ TO ME__   THE PART-ING__ GLASS__   GOOD - NIGHT   AND   JOY__   BE__   WITH YOU__ ALL ____

1. OH ALL THE MONEY THAT E'ER I HAD
    I SPENT IT IN GOOD COMPANY
    AND ALL THE HARM THAT E'ER I'VE DONE
    ALAS IT WAS TO NONE BUT ME
    AND ALL I'VE DONE FOR WANT OF WIT
    TO MEM'RY NOW I CAN'T RECALL
    SO FILL TO ME THE PARTING GLASS
    GOODNIGHT AND JOY BE WITH YOU ALL

2. OH ALL THE COMRADES E'ER I HAD
    THEY'RE SORRY FOR MY GOING AWAY
    AND ALL THE SWEETHEARTS E'ER I HAD
    THEY'D WISH ME ONE MORE DAY TO STAY
    BUT SINCE IT FALLS UNTO MY LOT
    THAT I SHOULD RISE AND YOU SHOULD NOT
    I GENTLY RISE AND SOFTLY CALL
    GOODNIGHT AND JOY BE WITH YOU ALL

3. IF I HAD MONEY ENOUGH TO SPEND
    AND LEISURE TIME TO SIT AWHILE
    THERE IS A FAIR MAID IN THIS TOWN
    THAT SORELY HAS MY HEART BEGUILED
    HER ROSY CHEEKS HER RUBY LIPS
    I OWN SHE HAS MY HEART IN THRALL
    THEN FILL TO ME THE PARTING GLASS
    GOODNIGHT AND JOY BE WITH YOU ALL

THE GAME OF CARDS

The Irish really do love their songs of romance and seduction. In this collection we have the wholesome attraction of "Heather on the Moor" and "Kiss in the Morning Early," the girl who won't take no for an answer in "Mary and the Soldier," and the bad seed in "Black Velvet Band." Here we have that rare seduction song that pits equal against equal (in such lovely, grinning metaphor that you can sing it to the most innocent of audiences). Do they both come out winners? You decide.

On the CD I sing the first half of the first verse, then immediately follow with the end of the last verse to show you how you can tie it up with a slight ritard at the end. Most recorded versions have slightly more involved endings. Possibly the most popular version is by the amazing Maddy Prior and June Tabor on their 1976 *Silly Sisters* album (Chrysalis 1101). On it, they finish up by lingering over the last line: "We'll play the game over and over and over and over again!" This album, by the way, is still available and an incredible source of inspiration, as Prior and Tabor are accompanied in turn by Martin Carthy, Martin Simpson, and Nic Jones, the three guitarists who defined contemporary British fingerpicking.

A couple of notes about the left-hand fingerings: First, starting with the fourth bar, pay attention to the unisons indicated on the tab line, either on the two highest strings or on the middle D strings. The unison fingerings serve both to accent the melody and to alter the open chord voicings. Second, you'll notice that the G chords are very insubstantial and the low G's are very fleeting indeed. Just try to hit them cleanly and then get off them again, as the implied chords and the sung melody will do just fine in carrying the underlying chord progression. For tips on playing D A D D A D tuning, see page 7.

AND THERE DID I____ SPY A BEAU - TI - FUL____ MAID -

- EN AS I____ WAS A - WALK - IN' ALL ON THE HIGH - WAY

1. AS I WAS A-WALKIN' ONE MIDSUMMER'S MORNING
   I HEARD THE BIRDS SING AND THE NIGHTINGALE PLAY
   AND THERE DID I SPY A BEAUTIFUL MAIDEN
   AS I WAS A-WALKIN' ALL ON THE HIGHWAY
   AND IT'S WHERE ARE YOU GOIN' MY OWN PRETTY DARLIN'
   IT'S WHERE ARE YOU GOIN' SO EARLY THIS MORN?
   SHE SAID I'M GOIN' DOWN TO VISIT MY NEIGHBORS
   I'M GOIN' DOWN TO WARWICK* THE PLACE I WAS BORN

2. AND IT'S MAY I GO WITH YOU MY OWN PRETTY DARLIN'?
   MAY I WALK ALONG IN YOUR SWEET COMPANY?
   OH SHE RAISED HER HEAD AND SMILIN' ALL AT ME
   SAYIN' YOU MAY COME WITH ME KIND SIR IF YOU PLEASE
   WE HADN'T WALKED ON BUT A FEW MILES TOGETHER
   BEFORE THIS YOUNG DAMSEL SHE BEGAN TO SHOW FREE
   SHE SAT HERSELF DOWN SAYIN' SIT DOWN BESIDE ME
   AND THE GAMES WE SHALL PLAY WILL BE ONE TWO AND THREE

3. I SAID MY DEAR MAID IF YOU'RE FOND OF THE GAMIN'
   THERE'S ONE GAME I KNOW I WOULD LIKE YOU TO LEARN
   THE GAME IT IS CALLED THE GAME OF ALL FOURS
   SO I TOOK OUT MY PACK AND BEGAN THE FIRST TURN
   SHE CUT THE CARDS FIRST AND I FELL TO DEALIN'
   I DEALT HER A TRUMP AND MYSELF THE POOR JACK
   SHE LED OFF HER ACE AND STOLE MY JACK FROM ME SAYIN'
   JACK IS THE CARD I LIKE BEST IN YOUR PACK

4. SINCE I DEALT THEM LAST TIME IT'S YOUR TURN TO SHUFFLE
   AND MY TURN TO SHOW THE BEST CARD IN THE PACK
   ONCE MORE SHE'D THE ACE AND THE DEUCE FOR TO BEAT ME
   ONCE MORE I HAD LOST WHEN I LAID DOWN POOR JACK
   SO I TOOK UP MY HAT AND I BID HER GOOD MORNING
   I SAID YOU'RE THE BEST THAT I KNOW AT THIS GAME
   SHE ANSWERED YOUNG MAN IF YOU COME BACK TOMORROW
   WE'LL PLAY THE GAME OVER AND OVER AGAIN!

---

*   THE PLACE NAME VARIES. PETER KENNEDY'S VERSION USES LEICESTER. FOLLOW YOUR BLISS.

A KISS IN THE MORNING EARLY

Irish singer Mick Hanly recorded two astonishing albums in the 1970s, *A Kiss in the Morning Early* (Mulligan 005) and *As I Went Over Blackwater* (Green Linnet 3007). Both are well worth hunting down for the bell-like clarity of Hanly's voice and for the easy confidence of his guitar playing. "A Kiss in the Morning Early," the title track of the first album, has always been my favorite Mick Hanly song. Such a universal story of young love and parental displeasure.

The song is sort of divided into four chapters; the first three chapters are two verses long and the last is three verses long. Accordingly, I end the first verse in each chapter (verses 1, 3, 5, and 7, plus verse 8) on a strong, unsettled A (dominant) chord, saving the resolution to the

D (tonic) for the end of the chapter (verses 2, 4, 6, and 9). I also like to play a full instrumental pattern ending on A between the chapters.

Much of the melody is played on one of the middle unison strings. I have notated the fingerings on the D string, although you could just as easily play them on the G string (tuned down to D). I find that I'm more likely to stay in tune on the D string. In the seventh bar of each eight-bar phrase, of course, be sure to bar the second-fret E on both unison strings together. Also note that I use my ring finger on the low G in the G chord at the beginning of the fourth bar, to free up the pinky for the higher G in the fifth bar. The ring finger stretch automatically kills the low A string, which is what you want here.

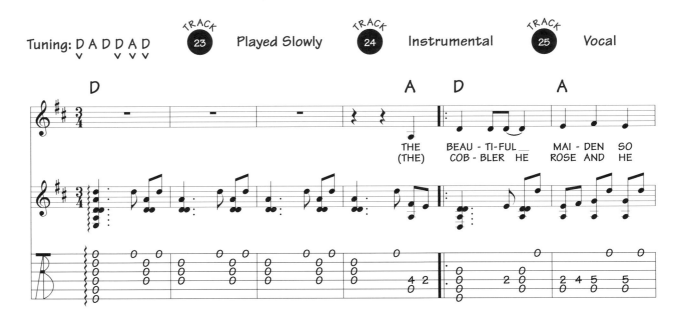

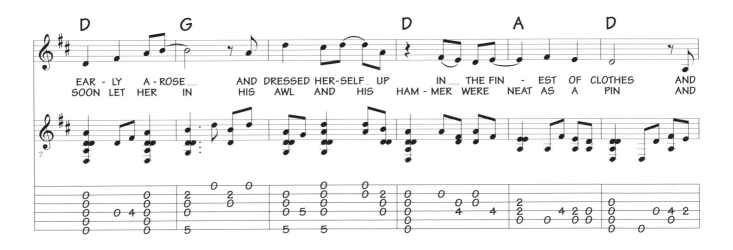

OFF TO THE SHOE-MAK-ER'S SHOP SURE SHE GOES FOR HER } KISS IN THE MORN-
HE HAD THE WILL FOR TO GREET HER SO SLIM FOR HER

-ING EAR-LY   THE EAR - LY

1. THE BEAUTIFUL MAIDEN SO EARLY AROSE
   AND DRESSED HERSELF UP IN THE FINEST OF CLOTHES
   AND OFF TO THE SHOEMAKER'S SHOP SURE SHE GOES
   FOR HER KISS IN THE MORNING EARLY

2. THE COBBLER HE ROSE AND HE SOON LET HER IN
   HIS AWL AND HIS HAMMER WERE NEAT AS A PIN
   AND HE HAD THE WILL FOR TO GREET HER SO SLIM
   FOR HER KISS IN THE MORNING EARLY

3. OH COBBLER OH COBBLER SO SOON WE'LL BE WED
   AND NESTLING TOGETHER IN A FINE FEATHERBED
   SO GIVE ME TWO SHOES WITH TWO BUCKLES OF RED
   FOR ME KISS IN THE MORNING EARLY

4. HE FASTENED THE SHOES AT THE BACK OF HER WAIST
   SHE PRAISED HIS GOOD COBBLING AND SHOEMAKER'S TASTE
   THEN OFF TO HER FATHER SHE MOURNFULLY PACED
   FOR IT WAS IN THE MORNING EARLY

5. OH FATHER OH FATHER I MET ME A MAN
   AND HE IS THE ONE I WOULD WED IF I CAN
   SO HANDSOME AS EVER IN LEATHER HE STANDS
   FOR ME KISS IN THE MORNING EARLY

6. THE FATHER WAS THINKING AND THINKING AGAIN
   FOR TO WED HER TO RICHES AND HAVE THEM FOR KIN
   WHO KNOWS BUT IT MIGHT BE A PRINCE OR A KING
   THAT SHE MET IN THE MORNING EARLY

7. WHO KNOWS BUT IT MIGHT BE A JOBBER FROM TOWN
   OR A WEALTHY SEA CAPTAIN WHO SAILS THE WORLD ROUND
   A MAN WORTH SOME THOUSANDS AND THOUSANDS OF POUNDS
   THAT SHE MET IN THE MORNING EARLY

8. THE FATHER WAS SMILING HIS DAUGHTER EMBRACED
   AND TOUCHING THE BUCKLES HE DREW BACK IN HASTE
   HE SPIED THE RED SHOES THAT SHE'D TIED ROUND HER WAIST
   FOR IT WAS IN THE MORNING EARLY

9. OH DAUGHTER OH DAUGHTER HE STARTED TO SHOUT
   WHEN HE DID DISCOVER WHAT SHE WAS ABOUT
   IT WAS NO YOUNG LORD JUST AN OLD COBBLING LOUT
   THAT SHE'D MET IN THE MORNING EARLY

MARY AND THE SOLDIER

This arrangement is based on Paul Brady's lovely setting of this song, recorded on the album *Andy Irvine and Paul Brady* (Green Linnet 3006). It sits perfectly in dropped-D tuning (with the sixth string lowered to D) and sounds nice either in D or capoed up to suit your vocal range. I capoed on the third fret for the accompanying CD, so I sing the song in F, though the tab shows the fingerings for D.

　　You shouldn't find the alternating thumb and finger picking pattern too tricky. And while I often like to slide up to the low G on the G chords with my ring finger, you can hit it straight on if you like as long as you maintain a nice, solid bass line with your thumb. One left-hand note: I tend to use my left thumb to cover the low B in the B-minor chord in the 15th bar. If this isn't practical for you, you should be able to get to a standard barred B minor from the preceding G chord if you don't worry about barring all the way across to cover the low string. Just barre the notes you're hitting and this little transitional chord shouldn't be a problem.

GAY___ THE COL-ORS FINE_ AND THE BAND DID PLAY AND IT CAUSED YOUNG MAR-Y_ FOR TO SAY_ I'LL

WED YOU MY GAL-LANT_ SOL-DIER

1. COME ALL YOU LADS OF HIGH RENOWN WHO WOULD HEAR OF A FAIR YOUNG MAIDEN
   AND SHE RODE OUT OF A SUMMER'S DAY TO VIEW THE SOLDIERS PARADING
   THEY MARCHED SO BOLD AND THEY LOOKED SO GAY
   THE COLORS FINE AND THE BAND DID PLAY
   AND IT CAUSED YOUNG MARY FOR TO SAY,
   I'LL WED YOU MY GALLANT SOLDIER

2. SHE VIEWED THE SOLDIERS ON PARADE AND AS THEY STOOD AT THEIR LEISURE
   AH MARY TO HERSELF DID SAY AT LAST I'VE FOUND MY TREASURE
   BUT OH HOW CRUEL MY PARENTS MUST BE
   TO BANISH MY DARLIN' SO FAR FROM ME
   BUT I'LL LEAVE THEM ALL AND I'LL GO WITH THEE
   MY BOLD UNDAUNTED SOLDIER

3. OH MARY DEAR YOUR PARENTS LOVE AND PRAY DON'T BE UNRULY
   FOR WHEN WE'RE IN SOME FOREIGN LAND OH BELIEVE ME YOU'LL RUE IT SURELY
   PERHAPS IN BATTLE I MIGHT FALL
   FROM A SHOT FROM A NINE-WAY CANNON BALL
   AND YOU SO FAR FROM YOUR DADDY'S HALL
   BE ADVISED BY YOUR GALLANT SOLDIER

4. I HAVE FIFTY GUINEAS IN BRIGHT GOLD LIKEWISE A HEART THAT'S BOLDER
   AND I'LL LEAVE THEM ALL AND I'LL GO WITH YOU MY BOLD UNDAUNTED SOLDIER
   SO DON'T SAY NO AND LET ME GO
   AND I WILL FACE THE DARING FOE
   AND WE'LL MARCH TOGETHER TO AND FRO
   AND I'LL WED YOU MY GALLANT SOLDIER

5. AND WHEN HE SAW HER LOYALTY AND MARY SO TRUE-HEARTED
   HE SAID YOUNG MARY MARRIED WE'LL BE AND NOTHING BUT DEATH WILL PART US
   AND WHEN WE'RE IN SOME FOREIGN LAND
   I'LL GUARD YOU DARLIN' WITH MY RIGHT HAND
   IN HOPES THAT GOD MIGHT STAND A FRIEND
   FOR MARY AND HER GALLANT SOLDIER

THE RAMBLER FROM CLARE

The version of this song included here is closer to the version I heard sung in Dublin pubs than to the version printed in Colm O Lochlainn's *More Irish Street Ballads*. It's also several verses shorter and leaves out the love interest, Sally Magee. O Lochlainn's version also shifts the narration of the story from the Rambler himself to the father coming to save him toward the end, but that always seemed weird to me, so I straightened out the point of view. There's something incredibly Irish about how this song stresses both dislike of authority and the power of family ties in times of trouble.

Tuning: D A D G B E   TRACK 30 Played Slowly   TRACK 31 Instrumental   TRACK 32 Vocal

1. THE FIRST OF MY COURTSHIPS THAT WAS EVER MADE KNOWN
   I STRAIGHT MADE ME WAY TO THE COUNTY TYRONE
   AND THERE AMONG THE FAIR MAIDS THEY USED ME WELL THERE
   AND THEY CALLED ME THE STRANGER AND THE RAMBLER FROM CLARE

2. TWAS THEN I ENLISTED IN THE TOWN OF FERMOY
   BUT WITH SO MANY MASTERS I COULD NOT COMPLY
   I DESERTED NEXT MORNING THE TRUTH I DECLARE
   AND FOR LIMERICK TOWN STARTED THE RAMBLER FROM CLARE

3. WHEN LIKE A DESERTER MY CASE TO BEWAIL
   I WAS CAPTURED AND TAKEN TO THE TOWN OF RATHKEALE
   THEN OFF TO HEADQUARTERS I HAD TO REPAIR
   AND IN THE BLACK HOLE LAY THE RAMBLER FROM CLARE

4. I TOOK OFF MY HAT AND I MADE A LOW BOW
   IN HOPES THAT THE COLONEL WOULD PARDON ME NOW
   THE PARDON HE GAVE ME WAS HARD AND SEVERE
   TWAS BIND HIM CONFINE HIM FOR NINETY-NINE YEARS

5. MY POOR, INNOCENT MOTHER GOT A WOEFUL SURPRISE
   AND MY LOVING BROTHER HIS SHOUTS REACHED THE SKIES
   BRAVE BOYS SAID MY FATHER YOUR ARMS NOW PREPARE
   AND BRING ME MY DARLIN' THE RAMBLER FROM CLARE

6. IT WAS THEN THEY ASSEMBLED IN A HARMONIOUS BAND
   WITH THEIR GUNS ON THEIR SHOULDERS THEY WERE TEN THOUSAND STRONG
   THE FIRING BEGAN WITH THE BOYS IN THE REAR
   AND THEY BROKE THE JAIL DOORS AND TOOK THE RAMBLER FROM CLARE

7. NOW I'VE GOT THE TITLE OF A UNITED MAN
   I CANNOT STAY HOME IN MY OWN NATIVE LAND
   SO OFF TO AMERICA I NOW MUST REPAIR
   AND LEAVE ALL MY FRIENDS IN THE SWEET COUNTY CLARE

ROCKY ROAD TO DUBLIN

This song may be one of the more difficult songs in this collection to master. First, it's incredibly wordy. Even if you can remember all the words, good luck finding time to get the next breath (actually, you'll find more syllables than you need in the version below—leave out any that seem unnecessary). Also, the song is in 9/8 time, also known as slip-jig meter, and that could take a little getting used to. If it seems alien, try saying "diddly diddly diddly" with emphasis on the first syllable. That's the slip-jig meter.

"Rocky Road to Dublin" is probably more often performed as a dance tune than sung. With that in mind, the arrangement here is really just the tune, fleshed out with some implied and fragmentary chords. When you sing it you'll be singing mostly in unison with the guitar, which can be great fun. And you get an instrumental session tune as a bonus.

Each verse is made up of a pair of four-bar phrases that repeat, followed by the five-bar chorus and as long a diddly-diddly D vamp as you like before the next verse. On the CD, you'll notice variations in the repeated phrases that may deviate a little from the written notation here. Not to worry. Hitting a different note in the arpeggio won't hurt a thing as long as you keep the rhythmic pattern grooving along.

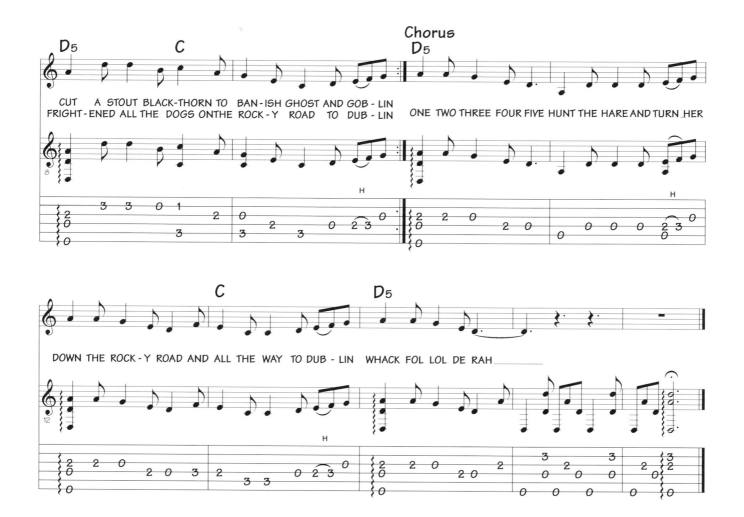

1. IN THE MERRY MONTH OF MAY FROM MY HOME I STARTED
   LEFT THE GIRLS OF TUAM NEARLY BROKENHEARTED
   SALUTED FATHER DEAR KISSED MY DARLING MOTHER
   I DRANK A PINT OF BEER MY GRIEF AND TEARS TO SMOTHER
   THEN OFF TO REAP THE CORN AND LEAVE WHERE I WAS BORN
   I CUT A STOUT BLACKTHORN TO BANISH GHOST AND GOBLIN
   BRAND-NEW PAIR OF BROGUES I RATTLED O'ER THE BOGS
   AND FRIGHTENED ALL THE DOGS ON THE ROCKY ROAD TO DUBLIN

   ONE TWO THREE FOUR FIVE HUNT THE HARE AND TURN HER
   DOWN THE ROCKY ROAD AND ALL THE WAY TO DUBLIN
   WHACK FOL LOL DE RAH

2. IN MULLINGAR THAT NIGHT I RESTED LIMBS SO WEARY
   STARTED BY DAYLIGHT NEXT MORNING LIGHT AND AIRY
   TOOK A DROP OF THE PURE TO KEEP MY HEART FROM SINKIN'
   THAT'S AN IRISHMAN'S CURE WHENE'ER HE'S ON FOR DRINKIN'
   TO SEE THE LASSES SMILE LAUGHING ALL THE WHILE
   AT MY CURIOUS STYLE 'TWOULD SET YOUR HEART A-BUBBLIN'
   THEY ASKED IF I WAS HIRED THE WAGES I REQUIRED
   TILL I WAS ALMOST TIRED OF THE ROCKY ROAD TO DUBLIN

   CHORUS

3. IN DUBLIN NEXT ARRIVED I THOUGHT IT SUCH A PITY
   TO BE SO SOON DEPRIVED A VIEW OF THAT FINE CITY
   THEN I TOOK A STROLL ALL AMONG THE QUALITY
   MY BUNDLE IT WAS STOLE IN A NEAT LOCALITY
   SOMETHING CROSSED MY MIND THEN I LOOKED BEHIND
   NO BUNDLE COULD I FIND UPON MY STICK A-WOBBLIN'
   ENQUIRING FOR THE ROGUE THEY SAID MY CONNACHT BROGUE
   WASN'T MUCH IN VOGUE ON THE ROCKY ROAD TO DUBLIN

   CHORUS

4. FROM THERE I GOT AWAY MY SPIRITS NEVER FAILIN'
   LANDED ON THE QUAY AS THE SHIP WAS SAILIN'
   CAPTAIN AT ME ROARED SAID THAT NO ROOM HAD HE
   WHEN I JUMPED ABOARD A CABIN FOUND FOR PADDY
   DOWN AMONG THE PIGS I PLAYED SOME FUNNY RIGS
   DANCED SOME HEARTY JIGS THE WATER ROUND ME BUBBLIN'
   WHEN OFF TO HOLYHEAD I WISHED MYSELF WAS DEAD
   OR BETTER FAR INSTEAD ON THE ROCKY ROAD TO DUBLIN

   CHORUS

5. THE BOYS OF LIVERPOOL WHEN WE SAFELY LANDED
   CALLED MYSELF A FOOL I COULD NO LONGER STAND IT
   BLOOD BEGAN TO BOIL TEMPER I WAS LOSIN'
   POOR OLD ERIN'S ISLE THEY BEGAN ABUSIN'
   HURRAH MY SOUL SAYS I MY SHILLELAGH I LET FLY
   SOME GALWAY BOYS WERE BY SAW I WAS A-HOBBLIN'
   THEN WITH A LOUD HURRAY THEY JOINED IN THE AFFRAY
   WE QUICKLY CLEARED THE WAY FOR THE ROCKY ROAD TO DUBLIN

   CHORUS

PADDY'S GREEN SHAMROCK SHORE

As an emigration ballad, "Paddy's Green Shamrock Shore" has maintained its power for well over a hundred years. It's been recorded countless times, but one of my favorite renderings is by Dolores Keane, on *Farewell to Eirinn* (Folk Freak 4004), a collection of emigration songs she recorded with her husband, guitarist John Faulkner, in 1980. In an era when we can cross the Atlantic in a matter of hours, it's hard to imagine that our emigrant forebears took weeks to make the crossing in cramped and dangerous sailing ships. If this song moves you, there are plenty more that tell equally interesting tales of hardship and human resilience.

As with "Black Velvet Band," part of the appeal of this ballad is that the verse and chorus are exactly the same melodically and structurally. (That's why only the chorus is written out here—the verses are identical.) It's not uncommon to hear the chorus sung first, just to set up the sing-along. As on "Mary and the Soldier," I capoed up to the third fret for the sake of vocal range. Rather than play this simply with a flatpick, I've added the little spice of some high notes played either in anticipation of low downbeats (giving the accompaniment a five-string banjo quality—see, for instance, the last beats in measures 20 and 21) or in unison with the downbeats (as on the first beats of measures 17 and 18). If you like, you can leave out these notes entirely, and the rest of the arrangement can be played either with a flatpick or the nail of your index finger braced with your thumb.

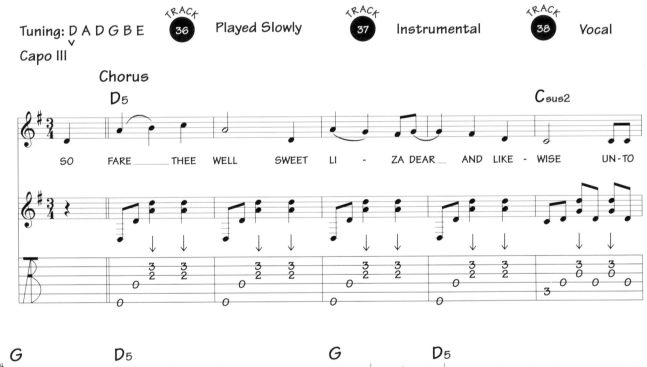

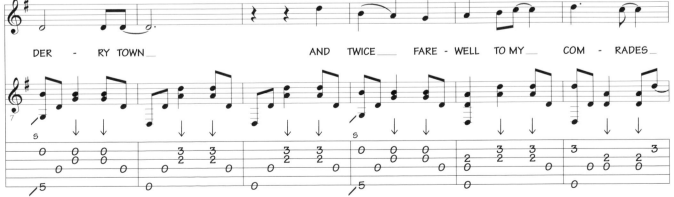

1. FROM DERRY QUAY WE SAILED AWAY
   ON THE TWENTY-THIRD OF MAY
   WE'RE TAKEN AS PASSENGERS ON A SHIP
   BOUND ROUND FOR AMERICAY
   FRESH WATER THERE WE DID TAKE ON
   TEN THOUSAND GALLONS OR MORE
   IN CASE WE'D RUN SHORT RUNNIN' DOWN TO NEW YORK
   FAR AWAY FROM THE SHAMROCK SHORE

      SO FARE THEE WELL SWEET LIZA DEAR
      AND LIKEWISE UNTO DERRY TOWN
      AND TWICE FAREWELL TO MY COMRADES ALL
      WHO DWELL ON THAT SAINTED GROUND
      IF FORTUNE IT EVER SHOULD FAVOR ME
      OR I TO HAVE MONEY IN STORE
      I'D GO BACK AND I'D WED THE SWEET LASSIE I LEFT
      ON PADDY'S GREEN SHAMROCK SHORE

2. WE SAILED THREE WEEKS WE WERE ALL SEASICK
   NOT A MAN ON BOARD WAS FREE
   WE WERE MOST OF US TAKEN UNTO OUR BUNKS
   AND NO ONE TO PITY POOR ME
   NO MOTHER DEAR NO FATHER KIND
   TO LIFT UP MY HEAD THAT WAS SORE
   AND MAKE ME THINK OF THE LASSIE I LEFT
   ON PADDY'S GREEN SHAMROCK SHORE

      CHORUS

3. WE LANDED UPON THE OTHER SIDE
   AFTER THREE AND THIRTY DAYS
   WE WERE EACH OF US TAKEN BY THE HAND
   AND LED ROUND IN SIX DIFFERENT WAYS
   TOGETHER WE RAISED A PARTING GLASS
   IN CASE WE MIGHT NEVER MEET MORE
   AND DRANK A HEALTH TO OLD IRELAND
   AND PADDY'S GREEN SHAMROCK SHORE

      CHORUS

NEWRY TOWN

This is a variant of the hugely popular song "The Creel," made famous by Paul Brady and included on his album *Welcome Here Kind Stranger* (Mulligan 024). I first heard this version in a Dublin pub in 1978, played with reckless abandon by guitarists Kieran Halpin and Mick Fitzgerald, with whistle player Johnny Keenan. It differs dramatically from the better-known version, but I think the chorus is unbeatable, especially as it hangs on the IV chord (a C chord in the key of G) until the very last repeat chorus to end the song. The plot is a little truncated here (though exactly as I first heard it sung), missing the final lustful romp that Brady's version sports, but still the lyrics get the idea across.

Playing "Newry Town" with a flatpick is a bit of a tip of the hat to Kieran Halpin, who was one of the true rockers of the Irish folk revival and who never got the notoriety he deserved. Also with Halpin in mind, I've capoed up to the fifth fret to sing in G, the key he sang it in. I've included the high D on the second string in the D chords, although I try not to hit it very hard, except during the "Too rye ah" chorus section. You'll hear on the CD that sometimes I leave it out entirely. And I like to keep my high E string open and suspended while rocking along on a D chord, leaving out that very sweet high F♯ at the second fret until the very end. Notice, too, that the last eighth note in the D and A chords leading to another chord are open G strings, though G isn't part of either chord. This allows you to switch fingerings without lunging.

By the way, when you've mastered this song in the D form, try taking the capo off and playing it in G while still in dropped-D tuning. You'll find dropped-D to be a very "G-friendly" tuning.

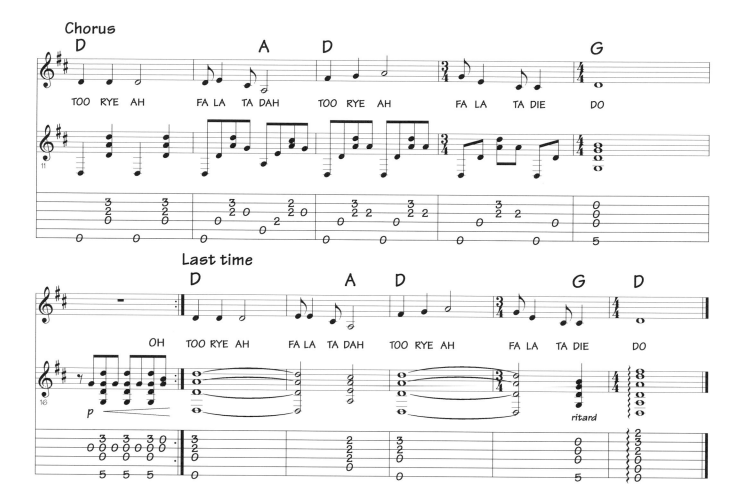

1. AS I WALKED OUT IN NEWRY TOWN
   SOME FRESH FOR TO BUY
   TWAS THERE I SPIED A BONNY WEE LASS
   AND ON HER I CAST A FOND EYE

   TOO RYE AH FA LA TA DAH
   TOO RYE AH FA LA TA DIE DO

2. OH HOW WILL I GET TO YOUR CHAMBER LOVE
   HOW WILL I GET TO YOUR BED
   WHEN YOUR FATHER HE LOCKS THE DOOR AT NIGHT
   AND THE KEY LIES UNDER HIS HEAD

   CHORUS

3. GO FETCH A LADDER NEWRY MAID
   WITH THIRTY STEPS AND THREE
   AND PUT IT TO THE CHIMNEY TOP
   AND COME DOWN TO THE CREEL TO ME

   CHORUS

4. NO PEACE NOR EASE COULD THE OLD WIFE GET
   WITH A DREAM RUNNIN' THROUGH HER HEAD
   I'D LAY ME LIFE SAID THE GAY OLD WIFE
   THERE'S A BOY IN ME DAUGHTER'S BED

   CHORUS

5. SO UP THE STAIRS THE OLD MAN CREPT
   AND INTO THE ROOM DID STEAL
   BUT SILENCE REIGNED WHERE THE YOUNG GIRL SLEPT
   AND HE NEVER TWIGGED THE CREEL

   CHORUS

6. NO CURSE ATTEND YOU FATHER DEAR
   WHAT BRINGS YOU UP SO SOON
   FOR PUTTIN' ME THROUGH ME EVENING PRAYERS
   AND I JUST LYIN' DOWN

   CHORUS

7. SO HE WENT BACK TO THE GAY OLD WIFE
   AND HE WENT BACK TO SHE
   SHE HAD A PRAYER BOOK IN HER HAND
   SHE'S PRAYIN' FOR YOU AND ME

   CHORUS

8. BUT NO PEACE NOR EASE COULD THE OLD WIFE GET
   TILL SHE WOULD RISE AND SEE
   SO SHE PUT ON A CHAMBER POT
   AND INTO THE CREEL WENT SHE

   CHORUS

THE GALBALLY FARMER

This amusing little tale of the dark side of nonunion labor is a favorite all across Ireland. I first heard it sung in Dublin in 1978 by Mick Fitzgerald in the legendary Slattery's Bar on Capel Street. His version was nearly identical to the one collected by Colm O Lochlainn in *More Irish Street Ballads*. To kick off the song I added the little instrumental tag, which I also like to use in between the verses, as notated here. My guitar arrangement here is a modification of the octave mandolin setting I've played for years.

Onstage with Caswell Carnahan, I'd use the tag pattern again at the end, leading into a jig in D. Oddly, recorded renditions of this song are rare, and the only one I'm sure of is my own, on the Caswell Carnahan album *New Leaves on an Old Tree*, long out of print as a Kicking Mule Records LP, then released briefly in 1995 on CD bundled with *Borderlands*. Stray copies of this CD can still be found by the stubborn Web-savvy collector.

Tuning: D A D G B E   **TRACK 42** Played Slowly   **TRACK 43** Instrumental   **TRACK 44** Vocal

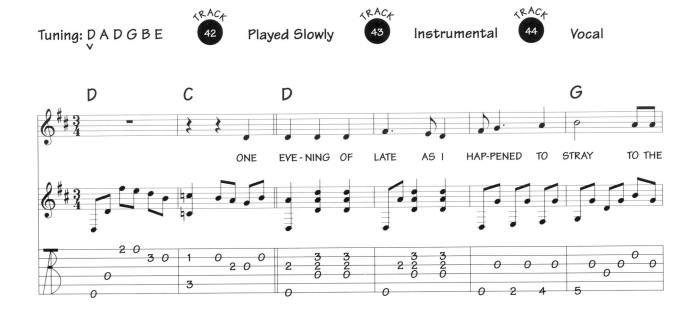

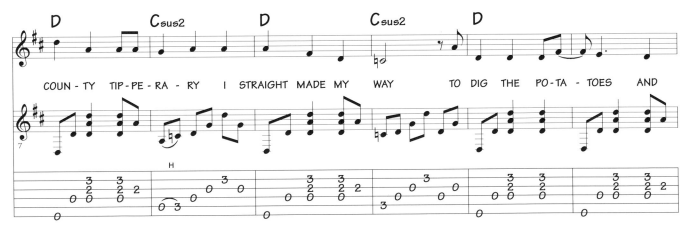

1. ONE EVENING OF LATE AS I HAPPENED TO STRAY
   TO THE COUNTY TIPPERARY I STRAIGHT MADE MY WAY
   TO DIG THE POTATOES AND WORK BY THE DAY
   I HIRED WITH THE GALBALLY FARMER
   WELL I ASKED HIM HOW FAR WE WERE BOUND FOR TO GO
   OH THE NIGHT IT WAS DARK AND THE NORTH WIND DID BLOW
   MY STOMACH WAS EMPTY MY SPIRITS WERE LOW
   FOR I'D GOT NEITHER WHISKEY NOR CORDIAL

2. THIS NIGGARDLY MISER THEN MOUNTED HIS STEED
   TO THE GALBALLY MOUNTAINS HE POSTED WITH SPEED
   AND SURELY I THOUGHT THAT MY POOR HEART WOULD BLEED
   FROM TROTTING BEHIND THIS OLD MISER
   WE GOT TO HIS COTTAGE I ENTERED IT FIRST
   IT LOOKED LIKE A KENNEL OR A RUINED OLD CHURCH
   AND SAYS TO MYSELF I'VE BEEN LEFT IN THE LURCH
   IN THE HOUSE OF OLD DARBY O'LEARY

3. I WELL RECOLLECT IT WAS MICHAELMAS NIGHT
   AND TO A FINE SUPPER HE DID ME INVITE
   A CUP OF SOUR MILK THAT WOULD PHYSICK A SNIPE
   IT WOULD GIVE YOU THE TROTTING DISORDER
   OH THE WET OLD POTATOES WOULD POISON THE CATS
   AND THE BARN WHERE MY BED WAS SWARMING WITH RATS
   TWAS LITTLE I THOUGHT IT WOULD E'ER BE MY LOT
   TO LIE IN THIS HOLE UNTIL MORNING

4. FROM WHAT HE HAD SAID TO ME I UNDERSTOOD
   MY BED IN THE BARN IT WAS NOT VERY GOOD
   OH THE MATTRESS WAS MADE IN THE TIME OF THE FLOOD
   AND THE BLANKETS AND SHEETS IN PROPORTION
   IT WAS ON THIS OLD MISER I GAZED WITH A FROWN
   WHEN THE STRAW WAS BROUGHT OUT FOR
     TO MAKE MY SHAKE DOWN
   I WISHED I HAD NEVER SEEN GALBALLY TOWN
   OR THE SKY ABOVE DARBY O'LEARY

5. I'VE WORKING IN KILCONNELL I'VE WORKED IN KILMORE
   I'VE WORKED IN KNOCKAINY AND SHANBALLYMORE
   IN PALACE-A-KNICKER AND SOLOHODMORE
   FOR DECENT RESPECTABLE FARMERS
   I'VE WORKED IN TIPPERARY THE RAG AND ROSEGREEN
   THE MOUNT OF KILFEAKLE AND THE BRIDGE OF ALEEN
   BUT SUCH WOEFUL STARVATION I'VE NEVER YET SEEN
   AS I GOT FROM OLD DARBY O'LEARY

HEATHER ON THE MOOR

This idyllic little love ditty is from the north of Ireland and was most famously popularized by Paul Brady, himself originally from County Tyrone. Brady recorded a great version on an obscure recording titled *The Gathering* (Greenhays 705), which also included cuts by Andy Irvine, Donal Lunny, Matt Molloy, and others. The late, lamented Flying Fish label licensed it in about 1981, so perhaps copies are still out there. My arrangement here is based on Brady's lovely little riff and incorporates pretty much every picking technique I've employed elsewhere in this collection. The only picking oddity is the pair of consecutive notes picked with the

thumb in the second bar of the vamp. The four-note ascending pattern will work with one thumb stroke and three fingers to follow, but the double thumb move gives it added drive.

In his book *Folksongs Sung in Ulster*, Robin Morton traced the origin of the song to a much longer story of a real-life Scottish courtship between a 62-year-old lord and a maid of 16 in the year 1681. True or not, the song is still popular all over the English-speaking world. The chorus repeats after every verse, taking the last two lines of the verse and using them as the third and fourth lines of the chorus, with the added tag line "And it's heather on the moor."

1. AS I ROVED OUT ON A BRIGHT MAY MORNING
   CALM AND CLEAR WAS THE WEATHER
   I CHANCED TO ROAM SOME MILES FROM HOME
   AMONG THE BEAUTIFUL BLOOMING HEATHER

   AND IT'S HEATHER ON THE MOOR OVER THE HEATHER
   OVER THE MOOR AND AMONG THE HEATHER
   I CHANCED TO ROAM SOME MILES FROM HOME
   AMONG THE BEAUTIFUL BLOOMING HEATHER
   AND IT'S HEATHER ON THE MOOR

2. AS I ROVED ALONG WITH MY HUNTING SONG
   AND MY HEART AS LIGHT AS ANY FEATHER
   I MET A PRETTY MAID UPON THE WAY
   SHE WAS TRIPPIN' THE DEW DOWN FROM THE HEATHER

   CHORUS

3. WHERE ARE YOU GOING TO MY PRETTY FAIR MAID
   BY HILL OR DALE COME TELL ME WHETHER
   RIGHT MODESTLY SHE ANSWERED ME
   TO THE FEEDING OF MY LAMBS TOGETHER

   CHORUS

4. WE BOTH SHOOK HANDS AND DOWN WE SAT
   IT BEING THE LONGEST DAY IN SUMMER
   AND WE SAT TILL THE RED SETTING BEAMS OF THE SUN
   CAME SPARKLIN' DOWN AMONG THE HEATHER

   CHORUS

5. NOW SHE SAYS I MUST AWAY
   FOR MY SHEEP AND LAMBS HAVE STRAYED FROM OTHER
   BUT I AM LOATH TO PART FROM YOU
   AS THOSE FOND LAMBS ARE TO PART THEIR MOTHER

   CHORUS

6. UP SHE ROSE AND AWAY SHE GOES
   AND HER NAME OR PLACE I KNOW NOT EITHER
   BUT IF I WERE KING I'D MAKE HER QUEEN
   THE LASS I MET AMONG THE HEATHER

   CHORUS

SOURCES AND SONGBOOKS

The following books are all reasonably easy to find, having been issued in various editions on both sides of the Atlantic. The editions noted are simply the ones I happen to own. While I used all these sources in preparation for this book, there are many other fine collections to interest the avid Irish music fan.

James N. Healy, *The Second Book of Irish Ballads*, 1968, Mercier Press.

Peter Kennedy, *Folksongs of Britain and Ireland*, 1975; American edition by Oak Publications, 1984.

Robin Morton, *Folksongs Sung in Ulster*, 1970, Mercier Press.

Colm O Lochlainn, *Irish Street Ballads*, Corinth Books, 1960. Also available as a Pan Books paperback.

Colm O Lochlainn, *More Irish Street Ballads*, 1965, Pan Books.

ABOUT THE AUTHOR

Danny Carnahan has been performing and recording Celtic music for over 25 years, playing guitar, octave mandolin, fiddle, and singing. Appearing in festivals and clubs from Scotland to New Zealand, he toured with duo partners Chris Caswell and Robin Petrie and shared stages with Celtic artists including Johnny Moynihan, Robin Williamson, and Johnny Cunningham. His recordings have earned two NAIRD Indie awards and one Grammy nomination. Carnahan's 11th and most recent CD, *Buckdancer's Choice*, is the second release with Wake the Dead, the world's first Celtic all-star Grateful Dead jam band.

Carnahan writes feature articles for *Acoustic Guitar* magazine as well as the regular Celtic column in *Mandolin* magazine. His travel writing has appeared in *Travelers' Tales* collections, and his series of Irish music mystery novels is awaiting publication. Carnahan also teaches songwriting and studio recording at Bay Area community colleges. He lives in Albany, California, with his lovely wife, Saundra.

Carnahan can be reached through both his website, www.dannycarnahan.com, and the band's site, www.wakethedead.org.

Hal Leonard Presents Guitar Instruction from

STRING LETTER PUBLISHING

The accompanying CDs in these book/CD packs feature all examples played slowly and up to tempo. All books are part of the *Acoustic Guitar Private Lessons* series.

INCLUDES TAB

ACOUSTIC GUITAR BASICS

CHORD AND HARMONY BASICS
By Dylan Schorer

This book teaches real-world chord voicings, shapes and progressions used by today's top acoustic players and provides valuable tips and tricks to help you understand and master the sounds of bluegrass, blues, folk, rock and roots music.

00695611 Book/CD Pack......................$16.95

COUNTRY BLUES GUITAR BASICS

Explore the essential sounds of country blues! In these ten lessons, you will learn the basics of blues fingerpicking, play some ragtime licks and cool turnarounds, learn walking bass lines, try your hand at slide guitar, and more.

00696222 Book/CD Pack......................$19.99

FLATPICKING GUITAR BASICS

Explore the essential songs of bluegrass and country guitar! These ten lessons teach the basics of rhythm, from the classic boom-chuck to bass runs and embellishments, as well as how to flatpick melodies and solos.

00696389 Book/CD Pack......................$19.99

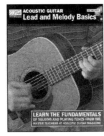

LEAD AND MELODY BASICS

Learn the essentials of playing melodies and leads in a number of roots styles, including folk, blues, Celtic and bluegrass. Includes lessons and 9 songs: Cripple Creek • Pink Panther Theme • Arkansas Traveler • and more.

00695492 Book/CD Pack......................$14.99

SLIDE BASICS
by David Hamburger

Hamburger guides players through this complete introduction to bottleneck slide guitar playing with progressive lessons in open tunings and fingerstyle technique, tips on slide guitars and gear, technical exercises, and full songs.

00695610 Book/CD Pack......................$17.99

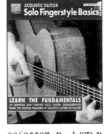

SOLO FINGERSTYLE BASICS

Learn to build simple melodies into complete guitar arrangements, understand fingerings that will bring intimidating chords within your reach, and learn country blues, classical techniques, Celtic music and more!

00695597 Book/CD Pack......................$14.95

TEACH YOURSELF GUITAR BASICS

This helpful book shows you the right way to play chords, songs and solos, with six essential lessons. Topics: Chords 101; Intro to Power Chords; 10 Great 4/4 Rhythm Patterns; The ABCs of Fingerpicking; Theory Made Easy; Your First Solo; and more.

00701232 Book/CD Pack......................$19.99

ACOUSTIC GUITAR ESSENTIALS

ACOUSTIC BLUES GUITAR ESSENTIALS

The 12 "private lessons" in this book/CD pack are full of helpful examples, licks, great songs, and excellent advice on blues flatpicking rhythm and lead, fingerpicking, and slide techniques.

00699186 Book/CD Pack......................$19.95

ALTERNATE TUNINGS GUITAR ESSENTIALS

Unlock the secrets of playing and composing in alternate tunings! Includes an introduction, 12 in-depth lessons in 11 tunings, 10 full songs to play, a special section on how to create your own tunings, and an extensive list of 60 tunings to try.

00695557 Book/CD Pack......................$19.99

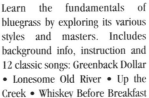

BLUEGRASS GUITAR ESSENTIALS

Learn the fundamentals of bluegrass by exploring its various styles and masters. Includes background info, instruction and 12 classic songs: Greenback Dollar • Lonesome Old River • Up the Creek • Whiskey Before Breakfast • and more.

00695931 Book/CD Pack......................$19.95

ESSENTIAL ACOUSTIC GUITAR LESSONS

This book/CD pack offers a superb selection of lessons and songs for the acoustic guitar. It includes exercises, licks and 8 full songs to play. The book is divided into four main sections: Basics; Rhythm; Lead; and Exploration.

00695802 Book/CD Pack......................$19.95

FINGERSTYLE GUITAR ESSENTIALS

Learn to build your technique, arrange songs, and use alternate tunings! Includes lessons by Dylan Schorer, David Hamburger, Chris Proctor, and others, plus 8 complete songs to play: Amazing Grace • Ashokan Farewell • Satin Doll • more.

00699145 Book/CD Pack......................$19.99

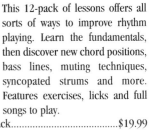

FLATPICKING GUITAR ESSENTIALS

Learn bluegrass and folk with lessons by Scott Nygaard, Dix Bruce, Happy Traum, and many others. Includes 16 complete songs to play: Banish Misfortune • Kentucky Waltz • Sally Goodin • Soldier's Joy • Will the Circle Be Unbroken • and more.

00699174 Book/CD Pack......................$19.99

RHYTHM GUITAR ESSENTIALS

This 12-pack of lessons offers all sorts of ways to improve rhythm playing. Learn the fundamentals, then discover new chord positions, bass lines, muting techniques, syncopated strums and more. Features exercises, licks and full songs to play.

00696062 Book/CD Pack......................$19.99

SWING GUITAR ESSENTIALS

Includes 5 full songs (like "Minor Swing" and "Avalon") and 10 in-depth lessons. Swing's essential styles and pioneering players are covered, as well as topics such as jazz chord basics, movable chord forms, swing soloing, and more.

00699193 Book/CD Pack......................$19.99